A 3-minute forever book

EAT YOUR PEAS™

for Grandkids

By Cheryl Karpen
Gently Spoken

To Ethan

With love from
Gram & Pop
2023

At the heart
of this little book
is a
promise.

It's a promise
from me to you
and
it goes like this...

If you ever need
someone to talk to
(really talk to),
someone who will listen
(really listen),
to what's on your mind
and
in your heart...

Call (or text) me!

I promise to listen to you
with all my **heart**,
all my attention,
and without interrupting.

What's more, I promise
to cherish you,
to lift you up
and
if I can help it,
never, ever let you down.

Here's my phone number
(just in case you don't already have it).

_____

*In the meantime,
there are some things I want to tell
you

like how important you are to me,
how I only want the best for you,
and how I wish you
happiness in life.

(Read often for maximum smiles and hugs!)

You will always be

grand

to me.

I'm so lucky.

♥

You are my grandchild.

The day
you were born
was one of the
happiest days
of my life.

I thought you
were one of the most
brilliant and beautiful
children born into the world.
And I still do!

I'll never forget
the first time
I heard you giggle.

It still makes me smile.

Do you know
how
happy
you have made me?

Happier than a double rainbow
in the sky!

Of all the gifts
I have received
in my lifetime,
YOU
are one of the
very best.

Every time I see you
there's a new memory
to tuck away in my heart.
How do you do that?

The future of our world
looks bright
because of *you*.

I'm so very proud of you.

Thank you
for reminding me of
some of the most
important things
in life:

Play. Laughter. Awe and wonder.

If only you could
see yourself through my eyes.

I see an amazing,
extraordinary,
bright, talented,
remarkable
YOU!

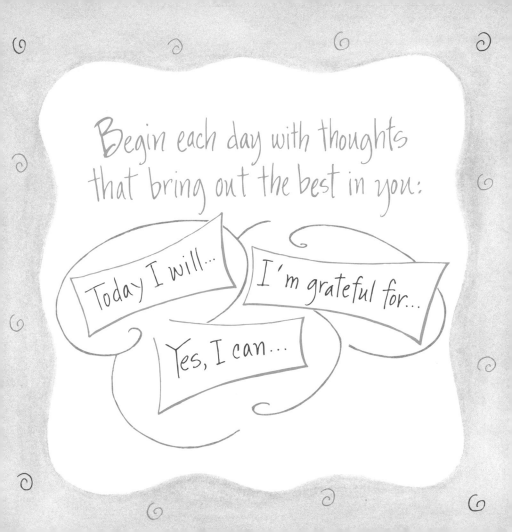

I
believe
in
you!

Grandparent wisdom:

1. Give yourself two hugs per day—
   one from me and one from you.

2. Be kind. Be really kind.

3. Ask for help when you need it.

4. Believe in yourself.

Try your best to
make good choices.

(They are much more fun to live with!)

Help whenever you can.
Whoever you can.

Helping others is good for your heart.

There is no challenge in life
so big we can't handle it
together.

Remember my promise...

I will always
be there
for you.

You will always be

grand

to me.

No matter what,
I will always
love you.

You are a very important
somebody.

It doesn't matter where you grow up,
what school you attend
or who likes you best.

One more time:
You are a very important somebody
and nobody, absolutely nobody
can take your
magnificence away!

Study hard. Play lots.

Be grateful for the little things.

Visit me often.
Whenever you can.

Dream BIG dreams.

Anything is possible!

You will always be *grand* to me.

Remember to always

eat your peas!

Love you
Gram & Pop
xoxo

With gratitude

A heartfelt thank you to illustrator,
Sandy Fougner
for sharing my dream and for gracing each page
of Eat Your Peas for Grandkids with her creative artistry.

To editor and friend,
Suzanne Foust
for being a joy to work with.

And to my sister,
Darlene Hauff
for sitting near the sea with me
and sharing her newfound insight into the
wonder and joy of being a grandparent.

I dedicate this book to my grandchildren:
Elowyn, Piper and Tadashi.
You light up my life.

Cheryl

A portion of the profits from the
Eat Your Peas Collection
will benefit empowerment programs
for youth and adults.

If this book has touched your life,
we'd love to hear your story. Please send it to:
mystory@eatyourpeas.com
or mail it to:
Gently Spoken
PO Box 365
St. Francis, MN 55070

About the author

"Eat Your Peas"

Cheryl Karpen was raised on a farm north of the Twin Cities
where she spent her childhood planting peas, **carrots**, and trees.
Not much has changed. Most days, if she's not
peddling her PEAS (to anyone that will listen), you can find her
with dirt under her fingernails dreaming up her next talk or project.

An effervescent speaker, Cheryl brings inspiration,
insight, and humor to corporations,
associations, education, and faith communities.
Curious? Reach out to Cheryl at
cheryl@gentlyspoken.com

About the illustrator

Sandy Fougner artfully weaves
a love for design, illustration and interiors
with being a wife and mother of three sons.

Other books by Cheryl Karpen

The Eat Your Peas Collection™

is now available in the following titles:

Birthdays	Extraordinary Young Person	Sisters
The Cure	Faithfully	Someone Special
Daily Inspiration	Forever Friend	Sons
Daughter	Mother	Teachers
Daughter-in-law	New Moms	Tough Times

New titles are SPROUTING up all the time!

Show someone YOU care!

Join the PEA-Volution on Instagram: @eatyourpeasbooks;
Facebook @ Eat Your Peas Collection;
Pinterest @ www.pinterest.com/eatyourpeasbook/

To view a complete collection of our products,
or to find a retailer near you,
visit us online at www.eatyourpeas.com.

Eat Your Peas® for Grandkids

Home grown in the USA

For more information or to locate a store near you, contact:
Gently Spoken
PO Box 365
St. Francis, MN 55070

info@gentlyspoken.com
Toll-free 1-877-224-7886